BEFORE I EVE
GRAND CENT
I SAT DOWN A

Front Cover: *Skyline from Queens*

BEFORE I EVEN GOT TO
GRAND CENTRAL STATION
I SAT DOWN AND WEPT

JOHN WARREN

Scorpion Publications

First published in 1979 by
Scorpion Publications Ltd
377 High St. Stratford London E15 4QZ

ISBN 0 905906 20 9

Editor: Leonard Harrow
Design and Art Direction: Colin Larkin
Illustration on page 14: Rhonda Larkin
Back cover photograph: Lawrence F Robinson
Set in Compugraphic Stymie 14pt
Printed on Blade Coated matt art paper 135gsm
Printed in England by Penshurst Press Ltd, Tunbridge Wells, Kent

for Ann

ACKNOWLEDGEMENTS

I would like to thank Leonard Harrow, Colin Larkin, and Henry and Mary DiSciullo for their assistance in the preparation of this book, and Eric Warren and Carmen Callil for their helpful suggestions. My thanks also go to Pan Am, the New Yorkers who gave me the right directions and those who gave me the wrong ones.

LIST OF PLATES

41	W42nd St.	1/60 sec. at f11, 65mm lens
42	Broadway	1/125 sec. at f16, 65mm lens
43	E47th St. and 5th Avenue	1/125 sec. at f11, 80mm lens
44	Pan Am Building	1/60 sec. at f8, 65mm lens, red filter
45	Greenwich Village	1/30 sec. at f5.6, 65mm lens
46	W31st St.	1/125 sec. at f11, 80mm lens
47	Broadway	1/30 sec. at f5.6, 65mm lens
48	Broadway	1/30 sec. at f5.6, 65mm lens
49	W42nd St.	1/30 sec. at f5.6, 65mm lens
50	Off Broadway	1/30 sec. at f5.6, 65mm lens
51	Chelsea Hotel, W23rd St.	1/30 sec. at f5.6, 65mm lens
52	Hotel bedroom door, W43rd St.	1 sec. at f22, 65mm lens, tripod
53	Wall St.	1/125 sec. at f11, 80mm lens
	Front cover: skyline from Queens	1/125 sec. at f8, 65mm lens, red filter

TECHNICAL NOTE

All the photographs in this book were taken on a Mamiya C330. Three lenses were used: 65mm, 80mm, and 180mm. The film used throughout was Royal X Pan and was developed in DK50 for 5 minutes at 68°F.

We're in Manhattan,
the Bronx, and Staten Island too. . . .

The photographs contained in this book represent the record of what is best described as a sentimental journey. This journey was in fact my first trip to New York. However, it was one that I had made many times before in the company of a very special group of people—the great stars of Hollywood. I had strolled along its great avenues and streets, and gazed at the famous skyline from the Staten Island ferry. For me New York was, and still is, a very special place. During the years immediately after the Second World War and in the fifties, when I was a youth and at a formative and impressionable time in my life, a whole barrage of images of New York was imprinted on my mind by means of what I saw in the cinemas around my home in suburban London. Thus during those years I formed in my mind a particular understanding and experience of this great city.

This image of New York was therefore shaped some time ago. It is a powerful memory for me and my own generation. Moreover it occurred during a period when attitudes towards what the cinema—Hollywood—was doing were quite different from those of today; likewise New York is seen today quite differently. With the decline in the great days of Hollywood, the change in taste of directors and producers, and the advent of television, the harsh reality of life in New York is the one that is now stressed. But for me this is not the image of New York that is the most vibrant. New York for me is still the New York of Hollywood, a whole concept created by those films I saw in the forties and fifties. From the present vantage point in time it is rather as if there are two distinct cities, but it is still the former in time, the old image, that exercises the greatest attraction and revives the strongest memories. For me this old image has matured with the passing of time and has hardened almost to the extent that it has become an era of myth, a distant golden age.

Coincidence finally gave me the opportunity of travelling to New York at the end of a long, dark winter. As a boy it had seemed such a distant place that I had never hoped that one day I might make such a journey. However, I was aware that I would not find it like the image of my dreams; there was no danger of trying to bathe in the same river twice. Yet the power of that Hollywood dream image was still so strong that I let myself hope that it might be based on reality and that I would find a magic and familiar city. It was a hope that did not last very long.

My first view of New York's amazing, graphic skyline was not the one I had expected. The great skyscrapers and canyons were still there of course, but they were obscured by tall chimneys belching smoke. This was the first indication that here there was not only another city at variance with that image formed during my tender years, but one that was far removed from it, possibly even standing in sharp contrast to the cherished image formed in the cinema.

I grew up in a dull part of South London. During the war years one grew accustomed to a stark landscape. One could open the front door one morning to find that the houses opposite had been blown away during the night by the bombing. There was in effect only one form of release and entertainment available to myself and my brothers—the cinema. During these years, and those after the war, to go to the cinema as often as possible was the main aim in life. There was no such thing as pocket money for us, so we resorted to whatever means were available to get together the pennies necessary to go into the cinema. We would chop wood and sell it as firewood, collect waste paper, or return jam jars and fizzy drink bottles for the deposits. With money thus gained we used to circulate among the three local cinemas, all extravagantly and aptly named—the Rivoli, Astoria and Ritz. Here were real magic lanterns, which whisked us away to strange and exotic places. As was common in London at the time, the local cinemas showed at least two different programmes every week; each consisted of a main feature, which was supported by the notorious 'B' film. Especially during the long summer holidays we achieved our hearts' desire and managed to get to the cinema every day of the week. By going to each of the three local cinemas in turn and catching the change of programme, one could see a different film every day. The main aim, once there, was to stay as long as possible; so by going in the afternoon we would see the programme begin with the 'B' film, then watch the main feature, and more often than not see the 'B' film through again before it was time to go home for dinner. Shortage of money to buy a ticket did not necessarily deter us—

one could always get in through toilet windows, or squeeze in through the exit doors as the first house was going out.

At that time it was often irrelevant to us what the film was or who the stars. Our aim was to be in the cinema and watch any film. Nearly all the films came from America and thus we were bombarded with Hollywood's view of the world. Because of the way in which we actually went to the cinema we were very much exposed to the world served up by the 'B' film. From the films we gradually put together in our minds a picture of America. However, this concept was never a complete one. Only certain strong images were stored away as memories.

Apart from the westerns, films set in places outside of America, and the numerous historical offerings, any film located in urban America meant for us New York. We had no understanding of distance or the geography of urban America. Apart from the Wild West we had no idea of the great contrasts of landscape or climate offered by the United States. Any film set in a city had to be New York as far as we were concerned. We were familiar with the areas of New York; we knew of Manhattan, the Bronx, Brooklyn and Harlem, but we never thought of Manhattan as an island; we certainly had no idea of the geographical relationship of the boroughs. There was never any notion that there was a New York State stretching away hundreds of miles to the north. In our minds New York was America. For us even the gangsters of Chicago seemed to operate in the streets of New York. Doubtless there were films set, say, in Boston or Philadelphia, but it would have made no difference to us—it would still have seemed like New York. Furthermore, the majority of plots and the stars of the great number of films I saw as a child are now beyond recall. I am only left with a vague impression of their faces and a familiarity with the urban America, i.e. New York, in which they moved. Looking back these are now memories of a golden era in my life, memories which have strengthened with the passing of time so that any reality has become indistinguishable from the myth.

My New York was a place of wonder where everything was as it should be, where everything worked. It was always efficient and clean. In many ways it was a strange place, for in contrast to us nobody ever seemed to travel by bus or train, one always went by taxi. These in themselves were wonderful things — they were always available, either instantly summoned by an immaculate doorman, or they screeched to a halt as soon as one raised a hand by the curbside. The cab driver was almost an institution in himself. He always knew where to go, was generally knowledgeable, wise and clever, was always civil and never acrimonious. He was never separated from his passengers by a thief-proof barrier. There was always an immense amount of room in the back of his cab, which was moreover fast and clean.

We remained effectively oblivious of the subway's existence, and indeed of the fact that New York had an extensive suburban area from which every day vast numbers of people would make their way to work in the big city. Such an idea was familiar enough to us from our knowledge of London, but the movies never saw fit to indicate that New York was so similar and hence even mundane and ordinary.

A number of films did portray railways. They always had the same destination — New York. The railway cars themselves would be enormous, with interiors lavishly upholstered and furnished to make them seem like New York apartments on wheels. They would have various rooms and servants to fetch food and drink; such men were almost invariably black, like the porters, servile and unobtrusive. The train would stretch for miles and be hauled along by a massive and magnificent engine. It would hurtle along the track day and night until it reached its destination at bustling Grand Central. The passengers of such trains were not ordinary mortals, they were actors, actresses and singers. These trains always brought theatrical companies or the casts of musicals to their inevitable success on Broadway. They seemed to cross thousands of miles of track, with the names of other towns an insignificant list of obscure names, but all the railway lines led to the same place. The great station itself never resembled anything with which we were familiar. It did not possess the same noises, hissing steam, general grime and scruffiness that we knew in London stations. Like every other place in New York it was on a vast scale with a wide concourse which seemed to have a surface of marble. The people around always had somewhere to go; they never drifted aimlessly, struggling with unwieldy baggage, and never seemed lost or mystified in the vast complex. It was also the place one went to in order to get a shoe-shine.

Like the taxi cabs, all the cars in New York worked perfectly. They were large and comfortable, sleek and shiny. They were almost an obsession with us, for the American car was outwardly a great contrast with the small, squat, almost chromeless and timid models we saw in our own streets. When it rained in New York — usually at night — the cars sparkled in the reflection of the street lights. The roads upon which they travelled were likewise perfect, they were as smooth as silk. Neither cabs nor cars ever seemed to become embroiled in any mighty traffic-jams, there were never any roadside breakdowns and the surfaces of the roads were never pock-marked or cratered. All vehicles glided along through towering buildings which always seemed to be hotels, offices or apartment blocks, all of which presented a clean, efficient exterior.

Anything mechanical within the buildings of New York was like the vehicle in the street in excellent working order, modern and of the latest design, for nothing in New York was ever out of date. The elevators in hotels and apartment blocks were silent and efficient. They always had an attendant who was youthful, smartly dressed, courteous and unblinking. The telephones were also remarkable, not so much because they always worked so well but rather because the party being called was always available at the other end and the lines were never engaged.

As well as having the external appearance which made it look to us a magic land, New York was always the place where anyone with any aspirations had to go. In New York there was all human life. It was populated by people who were never bored; life there was never boring. The whole city was never without a dramatic element so that someone was always going somewhere.

The people of New York were always reaching for fame and wealth, and that meant Broadway. Broadway seemed an enchanted place and nearby was 42nd Street. It was apparently a great street with vast areas of bright lights and neon signs. Here were all the very smartest theatres, cinemas, nightclubs and hotels. Nobody ever lived on Broadway, it was a place one went to to be famous, or perhaps one would go there to watch the stars, or as a star be watched arriving at the theatre or cinema in a very long, black limousine driven by an impeccable chauffeur. Broadway was the ultimate goal for all those who sought fame and fortune in show business and was the destination for all those 'the show must go on' movies. Tightly linked to the entertainment world it was in consequence a place that only existed after nightfall. For all we knew it simply disappeared during the day. The highlight of its nights of highlights was the first night. Musical film plots invariably led to a climax on this night. In spite of all the trials and problems getting to a Broadway stage, the first night was always a great success which sealed the good fortune of the show. The house would be packed with an elegant, enthusiastic audience of slick, witty and beautiful people.

Such people never seemed to live in little houses in the suburbs — New York had no suburbs. At rare moments one would peer into an ordinary home. However, it did not resemble what we were familiar with. New York never seemed to have a working class environment like that in which we lived. Within an ordinary home in New York were masses of consumer goods and gadgets. There were always ice boxes — the fridge had not arrived in our part of London — and vacuum cleaners. The rooms had fitted carpets and were centrally heated. All families possessed their own cars which were naturally big and modern.

The beautiful people would often live in magnificent hotels and their expansive foyers. These hotels were hives of activity. They were extraordinary places. Viewed from a scruffy post-war London they were New York's equivalent of royal palaces and there were a great number of them. They were invariably very modern with rich, lush interiors decorated in elegant art nouveau style. The furniture was luxurious and the carpets inches deep. Behind the front desk stood a platoon of elegant and handsome receptionists who retained total control of any situation and who were blessed with photographic memories of the guest list and room numbers. At the ready were swift moving bell-boys who conducted guests to their rooms. The rooms themselves were as gorgeous as the hotel's lobby, and as clean and inviting, even if they did seem to occupy the area of a football pitch; they were also usually suites and the bed would rarely be in evidence.

Like the wonderful hotels, all the apartments were New York apartments. They were contained in soaring, elegant buildings. The rooms were again spacious, even cavernous, and both furniture and furnishings were stylish and exuded success.

Such hotels and apartment blocks, which it was assumed were quite typical, were inhabited by as equally wonderful people. They rarely seemed to pay bills and never any rent. Their appearance was immaculate. The men wore hats and great square suits. Hair was carefully groomed and shoes always shiny. If anything the women appeared even more magnificent; there was never a hair out of place, they were invariably beautiful no matter what the time of day and had a staggering number of changes of fashionable and exclusive clothes.

Nobody ever went home to open a can of beans for supper. People usually ate out. They did not go into coffee shops or delicatessens, or even grab a sandwich, rather they frequented chic restaurants and clubs. They also indulged in something that to us as young boys was very mysterious — cocktails. In such places the food was excellent and the service attentive and swift. The bill was never a problem and the tip always adequate and gratefully accepted. Again there was a sense of great space, cleanliness and efficiency. Nobody was too poor to go to such places. New York was a place for people with plenty of time and money and such people as we admired were the only ones who ever seemed to exist in New York.

One was never quite sure where the money came from. There seemed to be remarkably little industry visible. Yet one knew the New Yorker was always busy earning money somewhere or other. At times one had a glimpse of business men at work. They were always successful in their transactions, working by telephone, dressed in their huge suits in prosperous offices down on Wall Street. Wall Street was a place only marginally less exciting than Broadway. It was also from such offices in Wall Street that business men astutely provided the finance for the great shows on Broadway. However, clean, spacious and busy Wall Street contrasted with Broadway in that it functioned during the hours of daylight.

It seemed to us that all the streets of New York were immaculately clean and tidy. In spite of the tall buildings on either side there was a sense of space and good order. The streets were long, straight and smooth, so that wherever one looked there was a vista flanked by hotels and apartment blocks, doubtless leading to Broadway or another important avenue whose name was one to conjure with.

The clean streets also had alleys which were occasionally to be seen. More often than not they provided the setting for a brawl amongst gangsters. Such garbage as might be stacked there would soon be sent flying by the sprawling bodies of fighting men. As garbage it seemed to consist mainly of paper boxes, and anyway was wholesome and convenient.

Advertising signs and billboards seemed only to be located on Broadway. Other signs on the streets were restrained and far from garish. They were never intrusive upon one's line of vision. New York was not the place where one expected to find posters plastered everywhere with tatty and peeling edges. New York's streets were tasteful in appearance, and of course there was no graffiti.

For us the only other type of familiar building in New York was the shop. There was not a shopping centre as such, just a store. The corner drugstore, owned by a friendly neighbour, was an Aladdin's cave. It contained everything. Moreover, if one wanted a packet of cigarettes, one never needed to specify the brand; the shopkeeper gave the correct one intuitively, although he rarely seemed to give any change. One never haggled.

Although I was probably too young to understand or notice anyway, there never appeared to be in New York those unfortunates that urban society is prone to attract. The flotsam of modern society such as beggars and down-and-outs were never to the fore in the images of my experience. At times there would be drunks, but not often alcoholics. Likewise there was never the hint of drug addiction, or the trafficking in drugs. In New York everyone had a useful purpose, somewhere to go and something to do.

An important element in the movies was crime and the officers of the law. The police were always tough but honest, and never in any doubt as to the course of action any situation might require. The cop on the beat had a particular appeal. We had our own Scotland Yard detectives, but our uniformed police always seemed to have little brains and big feet. New York policemen were the friends of orderly society and a part of it. Their uniforms did not force them to stand apart in a menacing attitude towards the citizens of the city.

Those engaged in crime pursued their profession with diligence, with important robbers often being portrayed as heroic figures. Nevertheless one always knew that the criminal would either repent of his ways or receive his just desserts.

There was never any likelihood of mistaking the bad guy. He was alwas a clearly identifiable type, as easy to recognize as the hero. The cause for criminal behaviour was always left as a grey area. He always had a kind and loving mother and came from a good home. The fist fights in which gangsters were involved — usually in those alleys among cardboard boxes — were clean and controlled. The fight was choreographed as carefully as a ballet. Fists would crash into flesh, muscle, teeth and bone. Such were the supermen involved that they never bled, except for the trickle of blood at the corner of the mouth; ordinary bruising was not for them although there might be the massive, shiny black eye to be soothed by a juicy steak. The hero was always attacked unjustifiably or forced to fight to defend his own or a lady's reputation. He never threw the first punch. The fight had its own rules: the villain could fight dirty, but the hero was not allowed to do so; instead he had to compete after the Marquis of Queensbury Rules. The movies' style of fighting and its code of behaviour even seemed to influence our own scraps in the school yard.

It is unlikely that my youth protected me from any aggressive sexuality in Hollywood's New York. It is more likely that it just never appeared. Certainly one was never aware of any explicit sex. It was above all a time of romance. If a male New Yorker became involved with a women they inevitably fell in love. This was regarded by us as an annoying sub-plot to the main action of the film. What they might do after the scene faded with a long, passionate, mouth-sealed kiss was never very clear to us. There were never idle women on the streets looking for men, and certainly no men on the streets looking for other men for pleasure or gain. Naturally no such persons were ever to be seen in the hotels, restaurants or clubs. The films remained wholesome and for all the family. Sex was always unseen, any implication always hygenic and sanitized, but there was love and romance.

In our New York there was never any indication that there were large groups of people who felt deprived because of their race or colour.

Any view of ethnic minorities showed them as happy and dignified. Even if poor — a rarity in itself — they retained their dignity and seemed happy. Like everyone else in the city they eagerly pursued those ideals of Waspish America that would also bring them in the fullness of time to success and fortune, although very few of them ever seemed to have achieved it. Such groups as the Bowery Boys for all their lack of obvious wealth retained a natural nobleness, humour and optimism, and managed to keep their faces clean at the same time.

There were no such things as militant blacks in my image of New York. They were all working, although most of them seemed to be grinning boot-blacks, or possibly cab-drivers, or wise old Uncle Toms. In any case there were remarkably few of them to be seen. Like all racial minorities they remained caricatures. There was no suggestion that they might feel themselves deprived. They were mere observers of the same image I was forming as a boy, it came from the same source and was the one to which we all aspired. In New York there was hope and optimism that each would eventually make his way in the world.

The New Yorker, and thus the American, was white and a beautiful person. The man was masculine, handsome and smart, and always tall. The woman was stunningly attractive and immaculate in appearance. Women often functioned as a decoration in what remained basically a masculine environent. Ordinary women rarely seemed to work for a living, except perhaps as hat-check girls or receptionists. It was only on Broadway as stars that women ever seemed in working terms to be the equals of men.

The picture created by the American film industry of its greatest city influenced our aspirations, to some degree our behaviour and often set the trends for our fashions. We wanted to be like the inhabitants of New York; at times a number of American words and phrases found their way into our everyday speech.

The stars' appearance and fashions seen on the screen led us to copy their hairstyles and modes of dress, The hair offered few problems, although we generally resisted the closely cropped crew cut. Clothes were a different matter for they cost money. However, we could always dream and look forward to the day when we would possess one of those ample suits and a gaberdine raincoat. For girls the movies dictated the way they dressed, did their hair and make-up, and made them obsessive about the straightness of their stocking seams.

As a back-up to the movies themselves stood the public relations machine of the studios. One would send away for autographed photos. Like the films themselves the photos were high quality prints, very carefully lit and heavily retouched, so that none of the stars we had seen strolling down the boulevards of old New York ever had the spots and pimples to which we fell victim. One also read the biographies of the stars, which showed them as rich and friendly, leading blameless lifestyles, and it always seemed they were writing directly to you. Girls seemed particularly susceptible to these influences, for the boys at least had some sort of counter-culture in the UK comic papers, packed with masculine adventures and excitement.

The New Yorker was always busy and creatively active. His job was interesting and successful. He never had a dull job behind a small desk, nor a monotonous one in a huge factory where he helped to make a part that went into something else that went on to make he knew not what. The New Yorker's job was responsible and important, he was a captain of industry. His life was hectic, but it had to be for his lifestyle exemplified the American work ethic. The New Yorker was also a little more; he was full of wise-cracks, occasional wit, yet hard-headed with that certain bite and sharpness that is acquired by urban man. Such bite is found in the people of many of the great cities of the world, but somehow like everything else in New York it was bigger and better. New Yorkers conveniently fell into clearly defined age groups. There were young people, the old and adults in their twenties and thirties. It was this last named group which came forth as the most important in the movies. Their education was of little interest, whilst their careers seemed to have little structure. By the age of 25 they had made it.

Art was little in evidence in this New York. People did not seem to read books, go to symphony concerts or visit the art galleries. When there was the occasional exception the movie soon showed him to be no less human than anyone else. The movies brought everything down to one popular level. The musicals it produced were light and undemanding, its dances were not classical but modern American, the jazz sometimes seen was usually that of the big bands, and any opera in films was confined to popular and famous melodies.

It was to New York that everyone wanted to go, to which all mankind seemed to aspire. It was a huge magnet that drew people not only from other parts of the United States but from all over the world. Its pull was irresistable. It attracted those who were already famous in other places and it also drew in those who sought fame and fortune. The new arrival would always come in by sea where the first sight of the great city from the deck of the luxury ocean liner would be that amazing skyline. Since its fame had gone before it, he would know for certain that in this city there was everything for everybody. Apart from offering whatever one might desire, it seemed that its climate was such that it occasionally rained, always snowed on Christmas Eve, and was favoured by long, hot summers.

This was the New York created in my mind after those many hours spent in the musty, stale air of 1930's picture palaces. It was of course an incomplete picture, in so far as my memory only chose to retain certain impressions and discard others. In comparison with the austerity of those years after the war when I was growing up, New York was the land of milk and money, and it was America. Those of my generation were great cinema-goers, and as a group we were subjected to a continuous stream of images and ideas emanating from the great days of Hollywood. We were seeing films from the thirties as well as from the forties, the good as well as the bad. Our image was a very personal one to a particular age group.

Since then things have changed greatly. Successive generations have not been such fervent patrons of the cinema. The convenience of television has replaced the cinema. The whole attitude of the media towards the world about us and the way in which it should be shown has changed almost beyond belief. There is no possibility that the generations succeeding mine will have such a vibrant image of New York. They are more likely to have pre-conceptions of a different sort which emphasize the badness of New York, its physical dangers on the streets, its crime, pockets of poverty and its lunatic pace.

For us things were very different. The effect New York had on us and the image we formed of it was probably similar to that made upon other parts of America as well as upon those in different countries. We always felt very close and at ease with America. The war as well as the natural bond of the English language thrust us into a close relationship with America, so that we knew as much about the United States — as seen by the eye of Hollywood's cameras — as we did about our own country. Its great political and social figures who had been projected onto the big screen became part of our own history.

We received most of our historical education through the cinema. What we were supposed to learn formally at school concerning the United States was rudimentary. At school American history formed only a small part of British colonial history. However, we knew that George III was mad and that his aristocrats needed money to fight the French. This money was raised by taxing the colonies in North America and the colonists' resentment led to the Boston Tea Party and the War of Independence. The Americans and their French allies won.

Whenever Hollywood dealt with subjects drawn from American history the actual issues were always simplified. The American Civil War became for us an important historical event, more immediate to us than many areas of British history. But the over-riding impression was of the tragedy of brother fighting brother. Slavery was merely noted to be a bad thing and the import of the Gettysburg address was never understood. The Civil War on the screen was dominated by the heroic figure of Abraham Lincoln or possibly by the name of John Brown. After 'Gone With The Wind' any image of that turbulent time was inevitably populated by the beautiful stars of the silver screen.

We had an awareness of the vast numbers of people who had emigrated at the turn of the century to North America from Europe. Often we had relatives who had taken that very course. Most immigrants for us would automatically achieve a higher status than that which they had left, and would step straight from the deck of the ship into an affluent middle class. It never occurred to us, because we never saw it on film, that America had slums and poverty such as existed in Europe, or indeed that there was really a working class as we understood it. Some groups of emigrants appeared to be destined for particular roles; thus Italians were to end up as part of the Mafia, and the seemingly small number of Jews in New York always became small shopkeepers.

Surprisingly we rarely seemed to see Chaplin movies. In many of these a background of poverty might have been in evidence. However, they were silent films and out of vogue, in which poverty and misfortune of social circumstances were the setting for comic escapades. Such films would have been considered, in any case, as a part of a distant age, and centuries away from contemporary New York.

New York at the turn of the century was ignored by Hollywood. We never knew of the work of Teddy Roosevelt or Jacob Riis. It was only many years later that the powerful work of Riis became known to me. Like so many others in America at the end of the last century, Riis himself was an immigrant, who was actually born in Denmark in 1849. In 1870 he went to New York and like so many others spent a number of years wandering around before finally settling down to work with the New York Tribune as a police reporter. The main police station was situated near Mulberry Street and the Bend, which were both terrifying and notorious slum areas. Riis was deeply moved by the misery and distress he encountered in these districts, and in consequence he undertook a crusade to draw the appalling conditions to the attention of the public and campaign for rehousing. In 1888 he decided to use the camera as an aid in his campaign and pioneered the use of flash photography in this context. His photographs were reviled as muck-raking but the scenes he depicted did have an important effect. He was a friend of Teddy Roosevelt who was mayor of New York at the time, and together they were able to pull down some of the slums and build tenements in their place. Riis recorded his work in his book 'How The Other Half Lives', which in its early editions due to technical problems did not contain photographs but only line drawings. The photographs of Riis remain as one of the foundation stones of photojournalism.

Although influential during his own lifetime Riis' work was gradually neglected. It has only been comparatively recently that his greatness has been recognized. To this day he remains virtually unknown outside of his adopted city. The state of parts of the city of New York at the turn of the century were never revealed to us. They were never a subject for the movies in our experience and Hollywood never suggested that in the

New York of our youth such sad and dehumanising conditions were a part of the American way of life. After all we knew our New York, and the people you meet on Mulberry Street, have you ever been there?

In a similar way we had very little information about America and New York between the wars. There was only the vaguest notion of the great events of the twenties. To us the idea of prohibition seemed great fun for it led to Capone and gangsters, who provided the basic material for so many 'B' movies. Even the problems created by the Depression made very little sense to our minds. In our situation financial ruin had no relevance; the Wall Street Crash merely conjured up the picture of people diving out of windows.

As children, and even as adults, there was a tendancy to accept as the truth whatever the camera happened to show us. We did not think that the camera was capable of lying. It was the apparent veracity of the camera that kept from us any distortion of the actual. However, what the Dream Factory chose to show us of New York did make available to us an avenue of escape. This was a huge part of its success, a factor which alleviated the humdrum existence of so many. For us in those dismal days, in a battered London after the war, the cinema was almost a narcotic. It not only projected us into a dream-like environment, but is also provided a hope of better things to come. At the time we were unaware of whether Hollywood had ulterior motives in creating the world as it did. It seemed of no consequence to young minds that here was not only a world full of wealthy, successful and happy people, but also one that demonstrated that the American way was the right and only acceptable way for an open society to function. All those films we saw as children were accepted as entertainment, which along with the desire for profit was the primary concern of those who made them. We were not concerned with looking for social comment or a 'message'.

Thus before making my first trip to New York I had gained from the films of Hollywood a whole range of vivid impressions of what the city looked like. Its landscape was as familiar to me as that of my own town. I also knew of its activity, its rush and bustle, the purposefulness of its inhabitants and their personal success. The first visit was in many ways a traumatic experience. I could not help feeling saddened to see stark contradictions to that image formed during childhood. I had suspected because of the new picture presented by the media that the city of my youth did not exist, but it was a thought more often than not shoved to the back of my mind. Yet here was New York; it was not as clean, slick and efficient as foreseen. Nor were its citizen all so usefully busy and active. I was to find that the ordinary hotels were no longer as luxurious and stylish, and that many of the residential areas were not endowed with such attractive apartment blocks. At the end of the winter the biting cold was such that people only went out if they had to, and no Hollywood film had ever conveyed the penetrating, freezing temperatures. Not all the motor cars were infallible and many of the roads on which vehicles travelled were in need of repair. Not every face was a handsome and beautiful one, and not every one was white and Anglo-Saxon. Broadway was not jammed full of chauffeur-driven black limousines, and I did not find myself rubbing shoulders with beautiful film actresses and tall, good-looking actors. New York itself looked as tired and dishevelled as any great city might, and like all great urban areas there was the persistent possibility of loneliness. At times New York also seemed to threaten the visitor; especially after dark the almost empty streets and the darkness might conceal a danger. The vulnerability of the individual was accentuated by the flashing lights of police cars and the howling of their sirens. The police themselves were miniature arsenals and in the back of one's mind one wondered why it was necessary and hoped never to find out.

Yet in spite of the knowledge gained by going to New York, and realising that the image which had resulted from so many hours watching films ought to be radically altered, the old memory remains intact and defiant. For me it is rather as if there are at least two New Yorks — there is the New York as created by Hollywood and the New York I found on going there myself. The photographs which follow portray a place which is not the same city I 'knew' as a child. This latter place is a concoction created thousands of miles away on the West Coast; it served as a scenario where the characters of the movies flickered across on the screen. The movie-makers' picture of New York was almost a convenience for their stars.

As a city New York is probably in many ways no worse than anywhere else. All cities have several faces, and all great cities — and this may be the greatest — have a side they would rather forget. They all have, as it were, an attic, where they can store all their unwanted junk. At the moment New York seems to have a lot of junk. In this respect it is no different from London, Paris, or any of the new, sprawling urban centres of the world. Yet New York is different in that it is still regarded by so many as the leading city of the world's most powerful and advanced nation. New York is the leader where others are sure to follow. To a far greater degree than anywhere else, and thanks mainly to the attentions of Hollywood, the face of New York has been paraded, eulogised and even immortalized. It has always had a less appealing aspect which has always been there and available for those who took the trouble to see it. It was certainly known to countless New Yorkers who lived in its less salubrious districts and may still be a reality to many in its present poorer parts. What Jacob Riis saw at the end of the last century was almost certainly far worse than what can be seen today. It is to the credit of New York and its citizens that especially recently it has been able to look at itself with a critical and discerning eye.

These photographs are to a large degree concerned with New York's less appealing face, certainly as far as its external appearance is concerned. However, they are not meant as a sneering glance at its citizens for whom I have nothing but admiration and respect. They themselves and history will always be in the position to challenge the cinema industry's view of the city. They know of the great robber barons who fed the tired, poor masses of Europe, watered and housed them, even abused and exploited them before propelling them on their way to fulfil the American dream.

These photographs stand at variance with what the movies chose to impress upon us. They are not really concerned with the massive area of middle ground which stands between the extremes. The middle ground is most of America and it possesses ample strength to look after itself. Like the view of the Dream Factory these photographs offer a point of view. Like the overall image that it challenges, it may be regarded by some as unfair, or even untypical. It is of course just as selective. However, these pictures are a true record of what a camera and a strip of film chose to see at a particular place at a particular time. Thus it may be argued that the end result is less artificial and nebulous that than produced by Hollywood.

It is also of importance to understand that these pictures not only contrast in subject matter with the movies but also in technique. From the films of my childhood, New York was also essentially a place coloured black and white and grey. If I close my eyes and think of New York, even today I still see it in these terms; it has never been for me an image conveyed in technicolour. However, the film-makers of Hollywood during its greatest years were the supreme practitioners of their art. The very film that they loaded into their cameras had high-quality, high-definition emulsions and was processed with fine-grained developers. The resulting pictures gave the finished product all the middle greys, and what was recognized as a quality look.

The subject was photographed through soft-focus lenses and was very carefully lit to enhance and emphasise the star. The subject itself was often in sharp focus whilst the background would be allowed to remain slightly out of focus. Consequently the viewer's attention was fixed upon the star, and the background was protected from close scrutiny. The same care was given to relevant publicity material and stills; in the latter particularly a portrait of a star would show a flawless complexion whilst the head itself seemed to be surrounded by a divine halo. After all, what else should one expect from a heavenly body?

In contrast to the style and technique of Hollywood, these photographs were shot on a very fast film and to avoid any excessive graininess were developed in a fine grain developer. Curiously enough rumour has it that the manufacturer produced this film for New York's police to enable them to quickly record suspects under adverse lighting conditions. As a result of using this film less attention has been given to the characteristic middle greys of Hollywood. The approach to the subject matter is also different; where possible the camera has gone back as far as possible to encompass the whole panorama, so that one's attention is not immediately and narrowly drawn to the centre of the plate. Again where possible the whole field of view is in focus so that everything can be seen from front to back. Although the photographs are carefully composed there is not the same emphasis on a particular subject in the centre of the viewfinder.

At the present time New York probably faces problems as serious as have ever confronted it throughout its astounding history. It has a series of local government problems, as well as economic and fiscal ones. It has its well publicized problems of crime and violence. There are also racial tensions, linked with unemployment and poverty. As elsewhere there have been changes in the make-up of its population and the sad process of inner urban decay. It has survived the great period of growth at the turn of the century, the strains of prohibition, the shock of the Depression and the attentions of Hollywood. It can, has and will survive any dent or assault. The city is the people as well as bricks and mortar. It can certainly take these photographs in its stride.

Many today would abuse the city and consider it a wilderness, but it still remains human and vibrant. Its harshness is that of the big city. The man who lives in and emerges from New York is the stronger for it. For its present generation it serves as much as a forcing ground for the greatness of the United States as it ever did, and probably more so than the plains of the West or the soft lands of California. It is New York that is the home of the brave.

Plate 1   Empire State Building

Plate 2   Harlem

Plate 3   Whitestone, the Bronx

Plate 4   Early morning commuters in the subway, Grand Central

Plate 5 · Chinatown

Plate 6   *Harlem at W123rd St.*

Plate 7   Tiffany's, just after breakfast

Plate 8   Shop window, W23rd St.

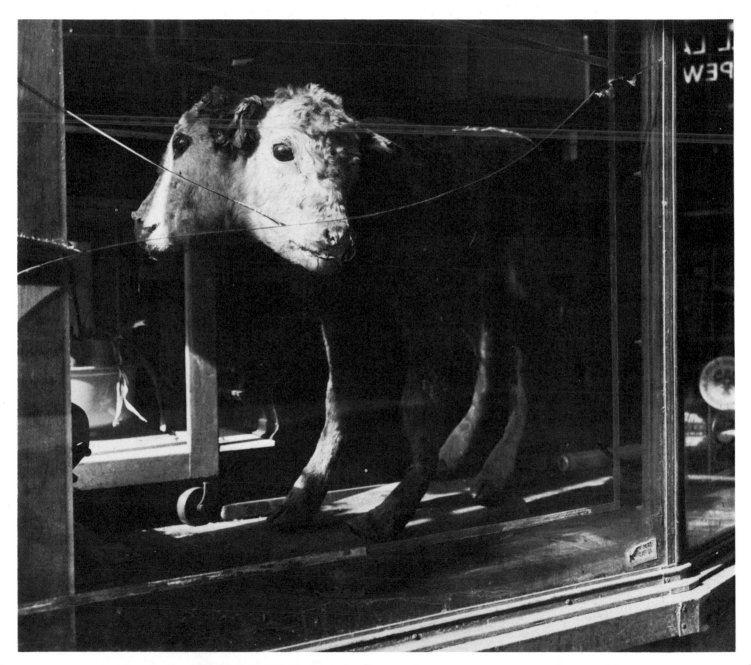

Plate 9   Penn St. Station

Plate 10   Macy's on Broadway

Plate 11   Taxi at Wall St. and Broadway

Plate 12   Automobile at W24th St. and Avenue of the Americas

Plate 13   Mulberry St.

Plate 14   The Bronx from the highway

Plate 15   W45th St. and Broadway

Plate 16   Cyprus Avenue and E138th St., the Bronx

Plate 17   W35th St. and Avenue of the Americas

Plate 18   Newsvendor, W23rd St.

Plate 19   Co-op City

Plate 22   1956 and 1957 models, Avenue of the Americas

Plate 23   Hotel, W43rd St.

Plate 24   Hotel, W43rd St.

Plate 25   Harlem, W118th St.

Plate 26   *The Bronx*

Plate 27 *New Yorkers dialling a favourite number, Avenue of the Americas*

Plate 28   Subway train, Yonkers to Times Square

Plate 30   Dealers and scorers, subway at Times Square

Plate 31   Zip-a-dee-doo-dah, Broadway and W46th St.

Plate 32   Adam Clayton Powell and W123rd St.

Plate 33   A captive in Central Park Menagerie

Plate 34   Off the leash, W32nd St. and Avenue of the Americas

Plate 35   *Fast working shoe-shine boy, Grand Central Station*

Plate 20 *The American Sugar Company, Kent Avenue and 2nd St.*

Plate 21   Hotel receptionist, W43rd St.

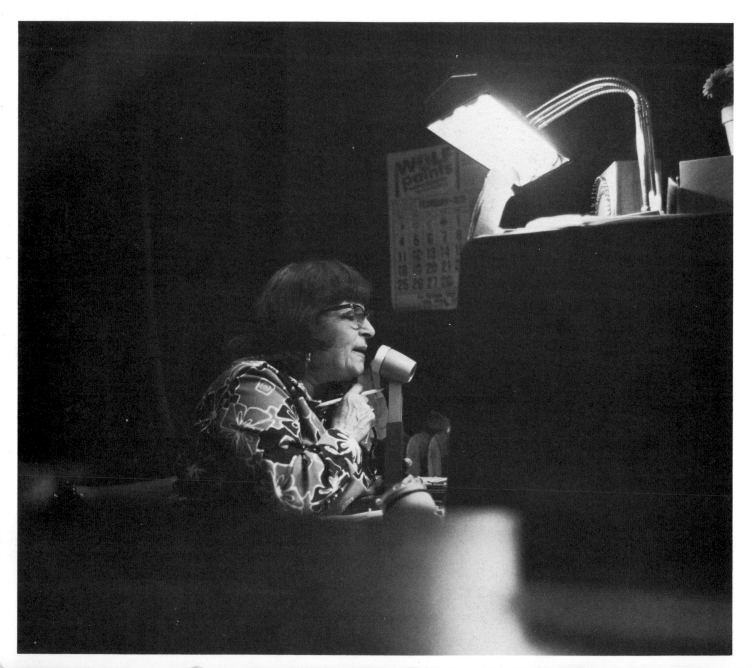

Plate 36   *Commuters in the subway at Grand Central*

Plate 37   Harlem

Plate 38   *W44th St. by Grand Central Station*

Plate 39   Broadway

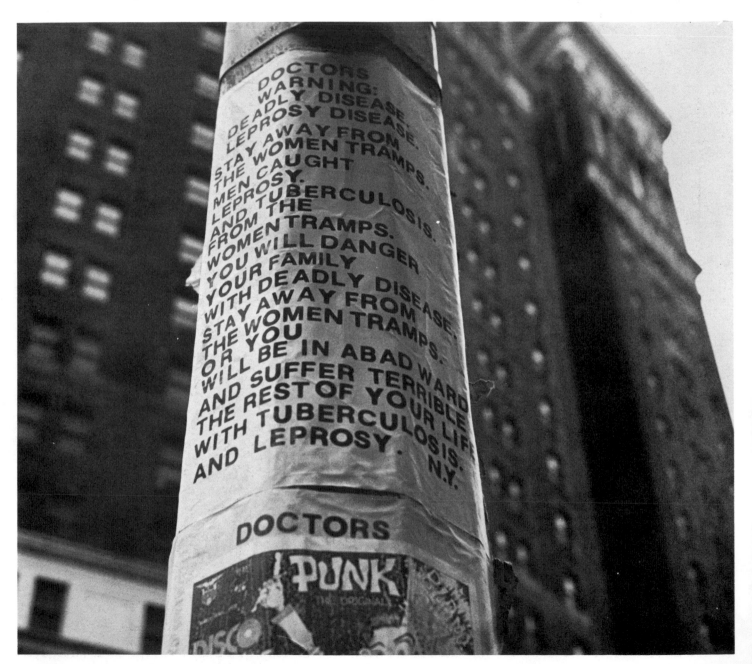

Plate 40   The milkman's on his way, dawn on W42nd St.

Plate 41   Big Apple screen spectacular, W42nd St.

Plate 42   Broadway

Plate 44   Pan Am Building

*Plate 45   After a rocking, reeling, rolling ride, I landed up
on the downtown side, Greenwich Village*

Plate 46   W31st St. The times they are a-changing

Plate 47   Broadway

Plate 48   Broadway

Plate 49   Welcome to 42nd St.

Plate 50   *Broadway Babies*

Plate 51   *Chelsea Hotel lobby. Staying up for days . . . writing*
Sad Eyed Lady of the Lowlands

Plate 52   W43rd St. hotel bedroom door

*Plate 53   Dawn on Wall St. My house shall be called the house of prayer;
but ye have made it a den of thieves*